ROUFLAQUETTES

– IAN BURTON –

FastPrint Publishing

www.fast-print.net/store.php

Rouflaquettes

ISBN 978-178035-488-0

First published 2012 by
FASTPRINT PUBLISHING
Peterborough, England.
Printed by Printondemand-Worldwide

An environmentally friendly book printed and bound in England by
www.printondemand-worldwide.com

FSC
Mixed Sources
Product group from well-managed forests, and other controlled sources
www.fsc.org Cert no. TT-COC-002641
© 1996 Forest Stewardship Council

PEFC
PEFC/16-33-415
PEFC Certified
This product is from sustainably managed forests and controlled sources
www.pefc.org

This book is made entirely of chain-of-custody materials

For Boris

Contents

Part 1

L'ange Heurtebise

(after Cocteau)

1.
Heurtebise descends marble steps,
Shot-silk wings unfurled, then
Sits astride me, brings me back to myself
Sharply; bad angel, frozen alone
In iridescent crystal,
Smashing my beast of burden's
Supernatural yoke and halter.

2.
Heurtebise with unheard of brutality
Leaps on me. Have pity,
Don't jump so hard, bestial angel,
Flowered statue with gilded mud eyes.
I'm laid out; what a way to treat me!
But I've got the ace of hearts.
You can see for yourself; but do you?

3.
Heurtebise pushes me off;
King Jesus have mercy,
Draw me up, hoist me, Father
To the sharp Merovingian right angle
Of your stone-draped knees.
Pax! Purest joy! Untie
These cords! I'm dying!

4.
Heurtebise, negative angel,
And Cegeste, killed in the war,
(Miraculous names) play
At being uniformed scarecrows,
Whose tattered and raggy "No!" terrifies
Each blossom on the cherry trees, under the reredos
Of the skies accustomed to a permanent "Yes!"

5.
Heurtebise, guardian angel
I'm keeping you to myself,
I crash up against you, startling speed changes,
Shatter you, change your space and time
Like someone changing stations.
Look out! Mauve lightning!
I'm warning you, if you're a man – admit it!

6.
Heurtebise, made-up with white lead,
Own up to your own beauty!
Demonstrated by this photograph
Taken with a magnesium flash!
Clothed in water, in a green-veil shower;
Grace punishes then deserts me.
I'm angry with God, and He's hurting me too.
7.
Heurtebise, this tortoise,
The demon spirit inside me,
Was once a plangent lyre.
Come down! Leave your white-laddered roof
Your crystal prison, with the speed which kills.
Become the drifting smoke
That solidifies into marble!

8.
Heurtebise, with your diamond skates
Scratch circles and stars on the mirrors
Of the dying; walls have ears,
Mirrors lovers' eyes; shoot forth
In an aeroplane rush of elderflower,
Snowy May blossom and lacy alabaster!
It's time, now! You've got to come down and help me!

9.
Heurtebise, dive head first
With your faultless vision
Through the mirror!
Burst through the void to this island
Where the fire sings gently on the hearth;
Take off your sword
And just slow down, frantic meteorite!

10.
Heurtebise, why haven't I got your body here, now?
If only I had your thighs, even draped with stone,
Wicked winged thing, loved by God!
On sky-and-leaf-spotted animal feet,
You arrived once while I was alone,
Beardless and naked,
Without Eve, no visa.
11.
Heurtebise, down here on the beach
The waves copy out a hundred times
The subjunctive of the verb "to love";
But I win! I win! As I brush against the nap,
The white-slubbed silk, of your newly-inflated
Diaphanous wings, and the pink, neon cross
Of the surgical dressing over the talking wound.

12.
Heurtebise, intercede for us,
Or just say hello!
One foot on the tortoise lyre,
The other on the great Swan's wing.
Look, I'm juggling here with feathers,
Stars and cannonballs!
I know I've behaved badly.

13.
Heurtebise, I was light-headed after all that fasting.
The earth's zebra light is divided,
One half sun, one half shadow.
No? Well I'm convinced of it,
So just shut up, and by the way
You've got blood
Trickling from the side of your mouth.

14.
Heurtebise, Sundays, Rue d'Anjou,
Plays and stumbles
On the roof against lurid orange clouds,
Limps and jumps
Rue d'Anjou hopscotch, a crow limping,
A magpie, slashed with turquoise silk,
Cheeks on fire
15.
Heurtebise, despite the radium snow
Be nice to me, glamorous cripple,
Half-naked glazier in your silver dungarees
They're spying on us so look straight ahead,
Hide your scissors, pearls, glass wings
Strapped to your back in a wooden frame,
They can't destroy you

16.
Heurtebise, because if they do
They'll also kill me
And I'm bulletproof!
Angel or fire? Fire-angel? Take aim! Fire!
He's fallen, shot by God's terrorists,
With a black snowball
Of compacted opium.

17.
Heurtebise, your death
Is the death of the seraphic,
The death of all angels
Much too mysterious a collective transformation;
The blood-red ace is missing from the pack
In the snowy dawn another angel has replaced him,
Cegeste!

18.
Heurtebise, I can hear the hollow
Beat of swans' bones in my blood,
Cegeste!
Is it a crime mingled with
Midnight's moon leaves?
Reveal your threatened hidden nest,
And the vine leaf concealing your immodest soul!

For Osip Mandelstam

Black
Hadrian coin, intricate gold seal
Stamped on this thick purple paper,
Degas' pastel purple
With an indigo frame beyond,
And curdled grey cloud
Lit within by mother of pearl
Above, and reflected by, the salt marshes below

Enamel
Bronze and bone cameo,
And the dark molten blue
Portrait of Claudius
Rising from the centre of a milky-gold,
Laurel-cinctured, glass plate,
Fragile and impervious space shuttle,
Hurtling through eternity

The idea of the one sumptuous book
Containing all the world, and the Word,
With its purple and indigo paper
And its cracked gold seal of Mithras,
Revealing the Resurrection as an ancient concept,
And in Latin the emblem:
"A small dog may bring a boar to bay,
For the weak may overcome the strong."

Ghost Koi

ghost koi
gold skeletons of fish
glowing beneath black scales

gold
then black
scarlet
white
swimming in the clear
black
crystal water

an art deco design
on a black lacquer plate

the ghost koi fins
the veils of Loie Fuller

Mozart In Paris

against the pale blue sky-cloth
whistling as you walk jauntily down the street
clouds painted also on the side of buildings
clouds
clouds
whistling as you walk down the street
in pale blue silk tricorne
and blue jeans
trying to work out the flute concerto

clouds on the sky-cloth
clouds on the side of buildings
whistling as you walk jauntily down the street
here with your mother in Paris
not long before she died
clouds
clouds
forever just walking with your mother
whenever the flute concerto is played

Lake Storm

Dense grey band of cloud
Molten magma-gash of dying sun,
Great cirrus swan's feather
Of burning brown-silver and bronze,
Colouring the water in flakes of grey,
Grey-mauve, bronze-mauve, lilac,
Pulsing together in molten pewter

With the black jetty sticking out into it
And from the black horizon,
Meeting the milky-green lake water
The flashing orange storm lights
On the shore, the unfurling apocalypse,
The thrashed foam, the terrible wind,
As the thunder smashes on the advancing wave.

Cairngorms

Cairngorms in the morning
Someone slowly waking from sleep
And totally covered with sheets of mist
Who throws them off
And half-emerges,
But then still half-asleep
Pulls them around himself again;

Lime-green chenille grass is nearest,
Then stripes of rust and docks,
Soft olive drift of birch trees,
Purple clumps of heather in islands
Separated by yellow grasses, pale blue hills,
And the mountains still covered in mist, detaching themselves
From the top, so that mountain becomes sky, sky mountain.

The Beggar Outside The Taschen Bookshop

The beggar outside
The Taschen Bookshop
And Orange Phone Warehouse,
Sits on a square of cardboard
And hides his face behind
Another cardboard sign saying
"S'il vous plaît
Une pièce pour manger,
Merci beaucoup".

Although he looks thirty
His real, arrested, age
Is only five, and like a shy five year-old
He waves and squints up his eyes
As I turn the corner of his street each morning,
His eyes sparkling and slightly frightened
Of the responsibility
Of doing us more good
Than we could possibly do to him.

He has children of his own, he says,
And therefore presumably a woman,
Although he doesn't talk about her,
And he lives in a caravan
Which, now it's January,
Has ice on the inside of its tin walls
Because he can't afford
The gas cylinders
Necessary to heat it.

Mnajdra

Close to the sea and its heat haze
The heel-shaped island
A special effect in the water

Now swarming with children
Who cling to the stones
Happy as lizards

Lintels and gateways
Stone pocked and pitted
With shallow holes almost Mycenaean

Like the big yellow butterflies
Open to the sun and sky
Turned nightly by the stars

Or at one time covered
With twigs and animal skins
Mud for pitiful protection

Hagar Qim

My skull is a stone
The flesh skin muscle
Covering the bone
Could be burnt away by the sun
Leaving it open
Like the circular ruins
To the cosmic life
Of sky moon stars and sea

The sickness has gone
Over-awareness of gravity
Being dragged into the earth
Air pressure

I can sleep here
Lose my self
And wake peacefully
See the light over the sea
The mauve clover
Yellow daisies
And palest gold white-bone stones
Through the long grasses

Into the labyrinth
Its apse with phallic pillar
The lintels the altars
Like pelvises pitted
And weathered with holes
Hear the permanent buzzing of the flies
Above the birdsong
The faint conversations of tourists
Visiting the ruins and the long
Scraping clicks of cameras

Lizards on the hot rocks
Fleshy grey vulnerable
Almost vegetable clutching the stone
The clean hot stone

Zurrieq

Not far from the cliff where bird catchers
Wait by stone piles, each topped with a cruel cage,
Is the old bar in Bubaqra, also a few hundred feet
From the Zurrieq Labour Club, and here sit
Fat ancient goatherds, and an ailing barman
Whose Socialist son is in the Catholic town band,
Arguing over the various traditional methods
Of cutting, binding and drying clover,
Now high and crimson and ready for gathering.

You see it through the door of the bar,
Over the dry-stone walls and the prickly pear,
From the hard mud floor, ankle-deep in peanut shells,
In this dark room sheltered from the sun, whose walls
Display nineteenth century colour engravings
Of a naked woman decoratively asleep,
Peered at in a forest by an armoured man,
Veiled in nicotine, encrusted with fly droppings,
Where old men and boys crowd into the shade.

Pareis, nick-named "Johnny Cash", grinning drunk,
Which he is most of the time, strums
Maltese folk songs on a matchwood guitar;
Walnut face, alcoholic twitch, cheered on by
Village boys who crowd in too, Johnny, Reno,
Franz and Charlie, one with his head shaved,
One blushingly handsome, who in the daytime
Stroll about lazily, just wearing jeans, past walls
Bulging and shattered by fleshy cactus.

In the rival bar of the Labour Club
Dom Mintoff's face rises weirdly from the waves
Next to the national emblem of a fishing boat,
Garish and stuck with the eye of Osiris;
Here it's all chrome, neon and bent Formica,
And the smarter boys here watch colour TV.
And the barman dreams of smack and Soho,
Porn and pimping, in liberal London, which he deems
"free";
"Is Malta free?", "Of course it's not!"

The television aerials on the outskirts of Valletta,
A frozen squadron of dead mosquitos,
Signal as in Sicily, social control,
And travel affirms this alienation;
Nothing is ever quite so clear,
Or as painful, we both reflect, as at home,
But painlessly I watch him play
For Hamrun Rovers, and meet him in the station bar
With his pale green linnet in its rat-trap cage.

The Man In Xaghra

His trousers are tied like a sack,
While arms, head and feet are bare;
He has a slightly crippled gait,
And two big yellow wolf teeth,
Though not in the least fearsome.

Something comes from him
Like the scent of the bean flowers;
He points to the sun, then to the ground,
Surely it's obvious, then over the valley,
And the scorched soil, to the sea.

His arthritic toes are the potatoes he digs.
He points to the sun, then to the ground,
Is amazed the connection between these realities,
And their proof for him of the power of God,
Is not immediate and apparent to everyone else.

His house has a huge hole in the roof,
Where birds flutter in the light;
He searches for a pencil and a piece of paper
On which to write the name of the shrine
Whose church, St. Joseph's, bears his name.

The tomatoes and root crops are not his own,
He works for a very large co-operative.
This doesn't worry him since he has few tools,
Mainly a small motorised plough
Which also doubles as a handy wheelbarrow.

His house is covered in white bird droppings
From pigeons and chickens tumbling through smashed
    rafters;
Also on the wall, going pale in the sunlight,
Postcards and photos of Australia, all of them
With a smiling young man.

The link between potatoes, tomatoes and the sun,
Between the photographs and the absent boy,
As well as the miracle-working shrine, embodies
All of his religion, and insists I visit Ta' Pinu,
A pilgrimage I have yet to make.

Hal Saflieni

The terracotta in the museum
of the sleeping woman

holds sacred her activity
inspired dreaming.

The hypogeum is the inside of a skull
in the hall with four chambers the water drips.

Stone steps on different levels
to the interconnecting passages of the cochlea.

Image of the inner life
of dream, imagination, prophecy and poetry.

The water drips in one cave pool
constantly changing note and pitch,

aleatory patterns
in the reflected torch light.
You can see the waves and ripples,
like watching sound, before your eyes close.

Childhood

In mine you could see
jockeys hunched up on a river of wind
through windows where birds were threaded on wires.

Then, along came love;
Madeleine with her pretty, squinting eyes,
and our fingers tangled up our sleeves.
Inevitably, she made me suffer
as much as it was humanly possible.

Then came the images,
wax and scissors,
wire heads which understood
the language of birds.
Playing children discovered
that statues at night
beneath their black gloves
hid powerful hands,
and glamorous Death,
on her high wire
cautiously showed me
her good side
then her bad.

Greece

Where both marble and sea
are curled like fleece
where knotted serpents
decorate a staff
where cruel birds
ask impenetrable riddles
where ships bristle
with thrashing oars
where shepherds battle
against rapacious eagles
where heartless incest
mounted on buskins
with its madwoman's cries
and plaster eyes
torments the theatrical
kings and queens
(Tell me if I'm getting
the style all wrong.)

The gods
(or rather the Devil)
have feathers and beaks
and also wear hats
made for flight
just like Mercury
gripping a numerical eternity
a figure of eight
on which he descends.

Deranging Angels

I have simply profited
from mysterious accidents,
celestial faults
in calculation;
this is the stuff
my poetry is made of.
I de-calculate the unseen
and print its traces.
I shout at vice
in its subhuman disguise,
"No more whining,
stick your hands up!"
I have given a contour
to the unformed seduction
of the tricks of death
(secretly informed
by the art of betrayal),
throwing my ink at them,
and turning phantoms
into shocked blue trees.
To declare straight away
that the enterprise is easy
would be sheer madness;
to say there was no danger
in deranging angels!
Discovering chance
learning to cheat,
or statues in the process
of trying to walk,

on the terraces of cities
apparently empty
(and close to the sea)
where all one hears
are cockerels and schoolboys,
and the horns of cars,
the solitary sounds
which mount from a town;
I have also heard falling
from the suburbs of heaven
terrifying cries -
a seraphic revolt.

Sudden Death

San Andrea della Valle died in church
In front of the altar, just like Father Odo Casel,
Although separated from him by three centuries;
The older saint celebrated in Rome, in the church
Where Tosca first met Mario, appropriately,
Has become the patron saint of those who die
A sudden death; the younger, chronologically,
In the practical examination of the Third Reich,
Celebrated the liturgy more rhapsodically
Than anyone since the early Fathers,
And who died, at dawn on Easter Day, in the chapel
Of the Benedictine nuns of Herstelle,
For whom he had laboured twenty six years,
Having sung the *Lumen Christi* in front of the altar
Three times, of a heart attack. 1948.

Thomas Merton, likewise, at the Red Cross Centre,
Bangkok, met a different death, though no less sudden,
Having visited the enormous Buddhas of Sri Lanka,
And Mahabalipuram, those vast smiles rejecting
 nothing,
And having delivered a lecture, very much of its time,
Like Pasolini, on the common ground between
 Marxism
And Christianity; and then in the afternoon,
Having taken a shower, was found dead, naked,
With an electric fan, burnt into his chest, still switched
 on.
Bare wet foot marks on the stone slab floor,

Then taken back to the Trappist Monastery
Of Gethsemane, just as he wanted.
Just before Christmas. 1968.

Wet rattan, naked light bulbs, the wet heat
Of the orchid forest, and the sudden casting of a soul
Into eternity; the open arm greeting,
In the accidental fall, padding from the shower,
Naked, drops of water on the conference papers,
The receptions, the embassies, the religious houses,
And now the soft, deep, red earth around the monastery
The bright green maize,
The big, plump, shining clouds,
The deep, high, azure
Sky over Kentucky.

Window

Oleanders going brown,
a milky blue-mauve sky,
new moon, one star;

The television flickering
soundlessly beneath the
dusty pink and ochre tiles;

The empty, blue-painted,
but lavishly flaking, swimming pool,
pencil cypress tree against the horizon

With its distant tower blocks
and now, only minutes later,
the pink and apricot, burning-newspaper-coloured sky.

And everywhere, as shrill as cicadas,
fat swallows performing their Grand Prix races,
under the eaves and round the open window.

Castell Coch

Fanned around Castell Coch
in Autumn, great fire-drifts
of scarlet and orange leaves.

Here one understands the High
Victorian dream, the dying swan,
the medieval fantasies of the richest man in England,

Of the hot and cold water taps
concealed within their little castles
and reflected in the crystal globes on the bed posts.

Serial Killers Haunt Our Dreams

Serial killers haunt our dreams;
in the frozen loft
of a deserted bungalow,
lit only by the blue flickering light
of a home-made pornographic video

with saws, bits of hose pipe,
and their kits for disposing
of the bodies; we know when they
look into their two-way mirrors
it is our faces they see.

Their monstrous anthropophagic desires,
and compulsions to crucify children,
are familiar to us not only
from the death camps that finally licensed them,
but in our ordinary rages.

Henry, Hannibal and Buffalo Bill,
in their lurid Hollywood afterlives
are a far cry from Edgar Lustgarten
(his name was carefully chosen too)
standing outside Rillington Place for the Pathe News.

Death In The District

Death goes to work in the district
Like a team of small-time burglars;
Two thin Irish boys in ill-fitting suits,
One limping, a plump black woman with
A baleful eye and too much powder,
A red-haired tough who's good at cars.

They move in and case the neighbourhood,
Notice the window a little ajar
To the widow's cache and her fragile life;
The faulty car lock and the steer spin
That careens it off the motorway
Into an ecstasy of flames and asphalt,
And the carelessly installed Ascot heater
Whose gas leak washes round the twins from Derry.

Stratford In The Thirties

Satin dresses the colour of the evening,
Chocolate box skyline of houses, with inset stars,
(A daring cutout of lavender and black)
Each with its keyhole porch, and in one garden
A rather avant-garde production of *The Taming of the Shrew*
In modern evening dress, the women wearing
Liqueur-coloured taffeta frocks.

Joan leans from her Tudor gable,
(Now a well-known tea shop in Sheep Street),
Unable to sleep in the summer night,
Watching the beautifully dressed men and women
Slowly drifting to the old Festival Theatre,
An anthology of Victorian Renaissance styles,
Before, like the first Globe, it spectacularly burnt down.

Birds

(after St. Jean Perse)

for Penny

Birds
of all our blood relatives
the most ardent for life
lead, at the confines of the day,
a singular destiny.

Migratory
and haunted
by solar expansion
they journey by night, the days
too short for all their activity.

In moonlight
grey as Gallic mistletoe
their spirits people night's prophesies,
and in the dark, their cries
are the holy and violent voices of dawn.

Under the flail
of their wings, they pass the huge
freedom of two seasons at once,
and, beneath the bow of their flight,
the curvature of the earth itself.

Alternation is their law,
and ambiguity their kingdom;
brooding over space and time
in the same flight, heresy for them
is a single summer's stay.

They share this scandal
with painters and poets, both
of them assemblers and collectors
in places at the highest
point of intersection.

Asceticism of flight!
Birds
of all our blood neighbours
are the most avid of being, and who,
in nourishing their passion

secretly carry
within themselves, the highest fever
of the blood, and the quickest heart-beat;
their gracefulness
is all in burning-up;

nothing symbolic about this,
merely a biological fact,
bird matter seems so light
that in the backlight of the first sun
it is shot to incandescence.
A man at sea,
scenting the noon,
lifts his head up to the
bewildering vision – a white seagull, wings
open to the sky, a woman's hand

against a lamp flame,
elevating to the light,
a rosy transparency, the dazzling
whiteness of the Communion host,
the sun behind its wings.

The boat pulled in
wings drenched in dreams
you will find us
this evening
on other shores.

The old naturalists
in their very precise and reverential
language, having given their due
to the attributes of the wing, the feather's
"staves", "quills" and "standards",

the "rectrices" of the tail feathers,
and all the "speckles" and "mail"
of the adult bird's plumage,
would attach themselves,
even more closely, to its body

and to the "territory"
of the bird itself, as though
to an infinitesimal
particle of our common
Earthly territory.
In its double allegiance,
Earthly and heavenly, aerial and terrestrial,
the bird is thus presented to us
for what it is, a tiny satellite
of our shared planetary orbit.

We would study, in its volume and mass,
the delicate architecture,
constructed for soaring
and the duration of flight, as well as
the lengthening of the sternum bone

like a ship's prow,
the strong chamber of the heart,
accessible only to the arterial flux,
and all the encagement of that secret strength
rigged with the finest tissues of muscle,

We would admire, like a Leonardo
drawing, this winged urn
in which everything
ardent and subtle
has been consumed

and to speed the combustion
of its interstitial system
as in a telegraph canister,
an arterial blood tree extending to
the vertebrae and wing tips.

The bird is carried
by hollow bones and air sacks
more lightly than straw,
and with the brilliance of its flight
defies all notions of aerodynamics.
The student,
or the over-curious child, who once
dissected a bird,
would keep forever the memory
of its nautical construction

and the ease
in which, in every detail,
it mimics a boat, with its thoracic cage
in the form of a hull
its assemblage of timbers at the keel

and the bony mass of its forecastle,
the stern or rostrum of its breastbone,
the pelvic belt where the poop is installed,
and the scapular belt where the oar
of the wing is attached.

The moment
of freedom has arrived
and more than the flight of birds
even, is this silent launching
of great painted images

like ships
on their launch cradles;
Braque whose fame was
the most enviable of all,
because his name

was born by a huge white
ship of the high seas,
a beautiful ship painted
layer upon layer in white
with six great diving birds
of the Arctic seas
perched on its prow.

Armenian Vespers At The Holy Sepulchre

"God hears all prayers at once"

"The Church awaits that day,
Known to God alone,
On which all peoples will address the Lord
With a single voice
And serve Him with one accord"

There are twelve choir men,
They are only just not boys, the age of disciples,
With strong, deep, sonorous voices, when
The procession starts, just to the left
Of the Stone of Unction.

The priest, an Archimandrite,
With his pointed black hood and luxuriant beard,
Intones the prayers and the passages of scripture
At each of the stations
Of this taper-lit procession.

The censer (who also carries
An ornate bell-rattle to focus
The act of attention at each sacred stop on the way),
Is bearded and dandyish in a lime-green and pink
Silk soutane with a black leather belt.

The young men process quite quickly,
Faces lit by the thin brown candles,
In each of the chapels, and in front
Of each altar they sing the antiphons,
Deep, nasal, and very loud, of the Orthodox Armenian chant.

We pass a group of monks and pilgrims going
Entirely the opposite way, singing Vespers in Latin,
But God hears all prayers at once,
And one by one we pray
In all the chapels of the Holy Sepulchre;

The Chapel of Adam and of the Invention of the True Cross,
The Chapel of the Angel and the Chapel of St. Longinus,
The Chapel of the Division of the Raiment,
The Tomb of Jesus, zealously guarded by other Armenian monks,
And the Omphalos – the centre of the world.

The twelve young men sing the office,
(Their brown-gold skin gilded by candles)
And in the Chapel of Golgotha, the site of the Crucifixion,
They line up facing each other, their lustrous black hair
Smelling sweetly of perfumed oil.

As the office and antiphons of Good Friday unfold,
One of the boys starts noisily crying,
Very visibly moved, as the others sing loudly:
"When Joseph, together with Nicodemus,
Had taken Thee from the tree

Thou who clothest Thyself in light
As in a garment, and beheld Thee dead,
Naked and unburied, that compassionate man
Was seized with weeping, and lamenting said:
'Woe is me, O sweetest Jesus, whom the sun

Beholding, hanging on the cross,
Clothed itself in darkness,
And the Earth did quake, and the Veil
Of the Temple ripped itself in twain;
Now I behold Thee, who for my sake

Of Thine own good will,
Hast endured death.
How shall I bury Thee, O my God?
With what winding-sheet shall I enshroud Thee?
With what hands shall I touch Thy body incorruptible?

What songs shall I sing at Thy forthgoing?
O Bountiful One, I exalt Thy sufferings!
In song I will glorify Thy burial!
In song I will glorify Thy Resurrection!
For Thou hast revealed Thyself as a stranger to corruption!'"

And I stand here at the foot of the cross
Listening to the Vespers, crying too, grateful to the singers
And the One they glorify, knowing something has changed forever,
Having bent and knelt under the altar
To touch the Rock of Calvary.

Cotehele

Drifts of wild white daffodils
flattened by the storms
like cow hide, round
the small flint manor house

Richard Edgecumbe,
leagued with Buckingham
(before he was beheaded);
swapped sides at Bosworth

to root for Henry VII,
threw his cap into the Tamar
here, with a stone in it,
to put his pursuers off the scent,

and later built a chapel
where he jumped,
dedicated to St. George
and Thomas à Becket.

The old ladies of the Edgecumbe
family retreated here,
while the more public
group transferred to Plymouth,

and so here are preserved
tapestries, old beds, with strange
dark red paper finials,
while the earliest clock in England

(which looks like a Tinguely sculpture)
resides in the chapel,
strange arms balancing weights
swaying and clucking while

a delightfully tinkly mass bell
strikes the hour in the courtyard
where the white camellias
cascade and rust.

One little courtyard
leading to another
like the rooms in the house
with their secret spyholes,

and a Victorian garden
with exotic trees
and a squat, mossed, dovecot,
tumbling down the hillside into the Tamar.

Doves, magnolias
white paper flowers
made by Japanese children,
primroses by wet slate
deep goldfish ponds
on the terraced slopes;
a Rowland Hilder Shell Guide
for the month of April

on the tapestries
Ovid by rural English
and Flemish weavers,
fountains, satyrs,

Orpheus and Eurydice,
how right the myth is
we shall not look into each others
eyes, when we are dead,

but we shall
pursue our journey
side by side,
gazing into the light!

Gardening, Mirfield

First things first;
in the early May sunlight
Mary's month
flowering blackthorn,
start the old galvanised tin
incinerator for garden rubbish,

or rather empty the ash
to put on the compost,
then open the greenhouses
to let in the clear air and light,
then inspect the bean sproutings
in their Indian encampment.

The gardener's boy's blonde thatch
is now kept back in a baseball cap
and he wears his shirt outside his jeans,
but he still tries boxing
against the creosoted wood
of the garden hut
I merely follow
the same instructions
to relearn prayer,
and watch from the wild fuchsias
growing in the stone wall
at the bottom of the kitchen garden

a fine sleek fat thrush
making little leaps
to pick off
small crunchy snails
and swallow them
whole

Malibran's Grave

Among the dust and cat piss smells
Of the Art Nouveau Necropolis,
In the shadow of the spot-lit basilica
Perched above the motorway,
Where the new Belgian monarchy
Are to outlast eternity,
And where Puccini briefly resided
Having died of throat cancer, here in Brussels,
And suffered the new indignity
Of primitive chemotherapy,
Crystal daggers stuck in his tongue,
A torture devised by Turandot

Is the little neo-classic temple-tomb
Of Maria Malibran, the first and greatest Norma of
  her age;
Nightly she emerges, dressed a little like
Mad Myrtha, Queen of the Villis,
Although still "girt with the mystic verbena",
Her druidic veils, stained with sweat
And old greasepaint, rusty and torn
By cats' teeth, her ankles bleeding,
She moves singing among the graves,
Where impressed into the soapy marble
Photographs of businessmen in their suits,
With their wives, dead in the Thirties,

Glasses, moustaches, in their cast iron
Neo-Gothic caskets, and the pale-green, withered
Plastic wreaths, now pulpy, looking as though
Chewed by a giant dog;
Children scream and play
On the War Memorial opposite,
Fragments of Bellini, as she steps
On the smashed stained-glass,
Trailing her dead Arum lilies,
The scandalous diva unknown on the edge of town,
Heard at night only, in the moon shadow
Above the whine of the speeding cars.

Trying To Keep Warm

Mozart and his wife
like "la cigale et la fourmi"
in one of their periodic bouts
of total insolvency,
were glimpsed through the window
of their tiny apartment in Vienna
(which hugged the cathedral),
dancing minuets
unable to afford fuel,
trying to keep warm,
dancing minuet after minuet,
trying to keep warm.

Rue Jacques De La Roche

Light on the cathedral tower
orange-grey storm sky
swallows diving hysterically
before a tornado, pink clouds
ripped across the sky
a crop-haired girl
thief, morphine addict,
sits on the collapsing high wall
above the oleanders
waiting for the rain
face towards the clouds
meditating on her confused life
meditating and waiting
in the rising wind

This morning there is a cool breeze
water dippers flip into the stone trough
in the garden seen through the tall
shuttered window in the white room,
ancient smooth-moulded plaster
thick white-painted cherubs,
the vine covering the old high wall
where the mad girl sits thinking;
watering cans, pigeons crawling
in and out of the grilles
where the spotlights point at the belfry
and the harsh voices of children
and cats fucking in the yard
of the cathedral primary school

Seven o'clock morning light
on the biscuit-coloured stone
of Viollet-le-Duc's restored belfry,
red birds tuck into the dark vine
flirt their coloured tails
next the arbutus and the Portuguese laurel
Naboth's vineyard desired
and coveted by Jezebel
the sun shines on the good and bad alike
the rain falls on the just and unjust,
love your enemies the tendrils say,
but first love the enemy in yourself
that desires the vineyard
and longs for Jezebel's blood

Apricots, cherries, redcurrants,
tiny sweet perfumed strawberries,
melons, salade de museau de porc,
boudin noir aux oignons,
brandade, taboule, pain aux neuf cereales,
all two minutes from my front door,
as well as the flower market,
dark red impatiens with green-bronze leaves
or pink with deep cerise-stained leaves,
oleanders, five different kinds of lavenders in pots
le paradis terrestre
young boys and women
with glowing skins like fruit peel
the bells say ever, ever, forever, ever

The tall open-shuttered window
of all the Matisse window paintings
filled with glaucous Portuguese laurels
bright pink and blood-scarlet
stemmed oleanders with long
dusty-blue spear-leaves,
on the sill a fringe of leggy,
translucent-purple petunias;
below, a lustrous vine on the peach
stucco of Saint Sauveur's outbuildings
and a brown pigeon perched
on a belfry gargoyle
while a man in his vest
hoses with a hissing spray

In The Square Of The Maynier L'oppède

Ten thirty on a summer night,
huge old plane trees
and a few pencil cypresses
peg out the area;

Little green metal park seats
on the ochre gravel, in front
of the four grand buildings
that form the square.

At nine o'clock on this summer night
a soft blue sky, the ghost
of the full moon visible,
a few pigeons tumbling and diving

As the crowd fill up to hear
Tomassi and Duparc;
gradually spotlights come up
in the shuttered windows

Somewhere the students tune up
instruments and voice,
swifts and swallows warble
as the orchestra assembles.

An old man tells the story of Tomassi,
dead in 1971, born Marseille 1901,
now forgotten by the French
although at one time all the rage

Ballets for Ludmilla Tcherina,
operas at the Aix Festival,
a guitar concerto in memory
of the assassinated Lorca,

The music irrepressibly Fifties,
a French *Red Shoes* composer, angular
like the cadenzas in this Clarinet Concerto;
while the swallows scream,

Duparc songs are sung by a girl with a fast vibrato,
"Songe a la douceur d'aller là-bas",
and slowly the moon rises
over the tiles, to drive us all mad.

Riesenrad

Get off the tram at the Prater,
Where Octavian used to ride
Through the oak-lined alleys,
Make towards the throb of the fair
In the last fierce sunlight
Before all the electric bulbs flick on
And the soft black night pushes in through the trees

And get onto the Riesenrad
With its boxed-in gondolas
Big as garden sheds, which go
Up and around and round and over,
High above the Imperial City
With Harry Lime's cheap sociology
And cynical attempts at self-excuse.

Perhaps we could live forever
In one of these revolving rooms,
And I could wash your vests and pants,
Cook Bosnian specialities for you, pies with peas,
Put flowers on the table in a jam jar as we go
Up and around and round and over
Until the sun goes down and the lights flick on.

Only later we could wander
Past the Ghost Train and the Donau Leap
(Black trees pushing in at the end of each alley),
Past the Bunjee jump and the Superman Ride,
The Big Dipper and the Tunnel of Love,
Then chat to all the ex-Jugos who run food stalls,
And shooting galleries full of stuffed blue bears.

La Petite Valise

Speaking of Rimbaud -
"Telle a été sur lui cette horreur,
Cette malédiction, a laquelle, comme Jonas,
Il a essayé d'échapper, par le blasphème
Et par la fuite, que… " (Genet continues)

"Hegijra… the Flight…
How does a journey start?
What pretexts are given?
What kind of love
Has germinated it?

In fourteen years my journey
Has led me through sixteen countries;
I have been through Jerash, and nobody knew me,
Before crossing the Syrian border,
Certain of finding nothing.

Now I have become a contemplative monk;
Everything is stripped down, renunciation,
Detachment, on my way (un captif amoureux),
To the Shatila camp in Beirut, after yet another
Massacre of Palestinians… the boys call me a Sufi saint.

I've become quite fragile with illness,
Like the time I was rejected by my mother,
And ran along the "thorn-strewn highway",
Humble, poor, broken by solitude,
Yet agile with curiosity.

Between nineteen thirty six and nineteen thirty nine
I travelled eight thousand five hundred kilometres,
Hitching, walking, riding on trains without tickets;
So by the time I wrote *Prisoner of Love*, I had travelled
Ten times the circumference of the Earth.

The man whose shoes were soled with the wind;
But there is only one place
That I would go back to,
Delphi, where the first shrine was constructed
From bees mwax and bird wings – and with Abdallah."

Genet stops speaking; the little case contains
A pair of beige-coloured corduroy trousers,
An old zip-up blouson with a fake fur collar,
An Arab book with a pale pink cover
Dirtied by rain, time and much reading,

A coarsely knitted roll-neck sweater,
A nylon shirt for quick washing, to change into,
A little toilet bag stuffed with drugs and pills,
And a copy of The Thousand and One Nights;
Once opened, the little case

Exhales a vaporous halo,
Hardly visible, inexplicable, harmonious, unexpected,
Like a distant mirage in the middle of the sand dunes.
After a few minutes, left abandoned and at rest,
It becomes like a blasphemous ciborium

Of his poetry which is a heightened vision of reality,
A sacred receptacle, and whose etymology
Goes back to the Greek for
"The fruit of the Egyptian water lily".
Still and always in flight… and to the end…

Part 2

Seven Highland Snapshots

For Anthea

1.
COVESEY BEACH

The sharp stink of seaweed,
And the scream of black-backed gulls
Rushes you back to childhood
Through the low grey cloud over the Moray Firth.

On one side the coastal path
By the cliff edge, leading through
The varieties of ling and bell heather,
And the purple, orange-brown and white campions,

The tough white seathrift,
And the quivering
Palest blue, butterfly silk,
Lantern-hanging, harebells

To where you look down
Over the free-standing arch of rock
Where the fulmars nest,
(Or just come to be lonely),

Onto the pebble beach, ground from
A hundred thousand different kinds of rock,
Speckled like birds' eggs, or with granite crystals,
Of violet, pink, black and white marble,

Bits of smoothed terracotta brick,
Kidney-coloured jasper, amber, chalcedony;
And on the other side the flat, wet, brown beach,
But a pinkish-brown like make-up in a compact

Stretching to the grey-purple
And pewter-green sea,
Under the low grey cloud
Of the Moray Firth.

Little flocks of birds cover
The water's edge; curlew, godwit
Drumlin and pretty oystercatchers.
But the beach stretches beyond the lighthouse

With its weird, white-painted
Egyptian features, past the palest sand dunes,
Tussocks of couch-grass
To certain, special black rocks

And reflected in a little rock pool,
Lined with white sand,
One veil-like piece of weed,
And one limpet
There
In the crystal-clear water
You can see the reflected image, and the shadow,
Of your seven-year-old self.

2.
OWLS IN THE CHIMNEY

Lying in bed, terrified,
You could hear them,
Four young barn owls, hissing,
And fussing over mouse bones,
Asthmatically breathing inside the chimney.

Then two builders,
One with USA on his sweatshirt,
Sandy-haired, bright dog-like eyes,
The other shy and handsome,
Tiny gold earring and a wicked broad grin.

Also wearing a white T-shirt
And navy-blue windcheater, squat
Astraddle the tiled roof-ridge as they attempt
To extract the owls using a clever length
Of two-by-one, with a bent bit nailed at the end

To hook the birds out,
From where they had bivouacked,
And then got stuck; three birds are sprung,
One by one, and with long-winged flight
They lope off to the birch forest

After their too-safe haven
Then enforced imprisonment;
The fourth is injured
And has to wait in the humiliation
Of a large stone jar and a cardboard box

For the RSPB to rescue him;
I think my mother saw the face of God
In the barn owl's stare, ferocious, protective,
And a silent magnificent hunter, hunting
The soul relentlessly, feeding its young

Under its breast, like the pelican
But using old buildings,
And never weaving nests, like the Son of Man,
Watching over the spirits of the dead,
White face hovering, silently, over the Moravian graveyard.

3.
TO THE NATURAL SWIMMING POOL

Dun
Mountain, blue mountain
Purple mountain

White sheep
White boulder
White sheep skull

The heather
A violet ocean
Broad wave upon wave

Of the paler
Ling and the deeper
Purple bell heather

And the heather
Whose flowers have dried in death
To a russet of rich orange-brown.

On the path
Through the mountains, past the
Ruined croft, a pile of granite rubble.

Black-faced
White sheep, against
The Derain swathes of purple

And one pine
With blue-green, brushed-up branches
In the light rain, the emerald singing

Against
The purple surf, and the burn
Snaking along the valley bottom

Over
Weed-strewn rocks, broad
Arrow shapes of lime-green hair

Smoothed-out
In the dark, clear water
Up to the great dog-headed boulder

Past
Waterfalls of chunnelling,
Musically gurgling, white water

And twisted
Pines, tumbling down
The ravine, to the Natural Swimming Pool.

4.
LACHLAN STEWART

Tall, gangling, Highland Scot,
Although in his thirties, a rather fey boy

But with very big shoes, and sticky out hair
That he must cut himself

Endlessly enthusiastic about the house
And the variety of Highland vernacular building

Sharing Dougal's accent of pure stream water,
Very measured and almost pedantic,

And, of course, wearing
Very pale green Stewart tweeds.

5.
ATTINLEA

Two or three crofts, outhouses
And a barn, tied together by a tower,
Tiled with oatmeal and with lumps
Of coagulated granite poking out,

Like the stone of the old farm buildings,
Grey, pinkish-brown and ancient
As the half-buried boulders casually thrown
On the sides of the niveated river valley,

Now covered in soft, green fur
Under birch trees, or in streams
Overlooking the Cairngorms;
From the water meadows in front of them

The endlessly changing light
Plays across the dried-mustard chenille cloth,
Mildewed gold and dusty-purple, pulled
In swathes and draped over the boggy plain.

6.
ARDCLACH BELL TOWER

The road suddenly dips down to the river,
And the church sits on the flat meadow
Where the broad, black, Findhorn bends.

The church is bare but beautiful,
Windows mysteriously boarded up
And Highland Baroque head-stones in the churchyard.

The bell tower on the cliff above
Perfect, modern as Mackintosh, small high-up
Windows, steeped in Covenanters' blood.

High pine and birch-clad cliffs on every side
With big wild salmon leaping from the flat water
The colour of the darkest malt Macallan.

7.
STILL LIFE

"Haw daw meddle wi' me?"
Says the spiked hand grenade of the thistle,
The medieval spikes, spines and leaves spoke,
Not the soft purple crown of stamens.

"Not anymore," answered the dead,
Fly-blown rabbit, with black oil pools
And a swarm of grubs for eyes;
"Nor me," said the dead, black-faced sheep

Trying to bury itself in the purple bell heather,
Digging with its hard-ridged horns,
Its huge rump, brown as dirty snow, about
To explode with the gas of its own decomposition.

8.
FROM A BIRCH SEAT

In the Birchwood
the light is speckled;
early gold medallions
dot the ground

round the huge granite
boulder, Tolstoy's tomb,
surrounded by a path
of split birch boughs;

house and tower
on the edge of the copse
looking over to Roumania
across the vast plain,
grain of birch slats
for the seat, and beyond
Meall a' Bhuachaille
Einich Cairn and Ben Macdui

Touill Cairn and Braig Riabhach;
in the far blue distance
Creagan Gorm and the other
Cairngorm peaks

streaks of seven o'clock
pale gold-pink light
strike the side of the tower
and the tiny windows

groves of smaller, feathery
bronze-leafed birches
encincture the granite crofts
while vast cloudscapes above

shift piles of gold and orange
corn-cob sacks, gaps of indigo
distance, before digging up
potatoes in the bothy yard.

Study

In front of one window
Which gives onto snow-walled gardens
And trees, thick with opium blue
Blurring the edges of everything,
Is a large white orchid, whose many stems
Detail flowers in successive stages, from
Fine-boned cat mouth to ivory carved bird skull,
Greenish at the centre, a tiny iceberg,
Like the successive arias of *Norma* playing
In the library, alike yet subtly different,
"Lunge, lunge, lunge melodie," slowly
And exquisitely growing out of each other,
In the study walled with fruit wood
And a resin-spurting fire, soft pyramids
Of orange-purring flame, and above, a painting
Of a melancholy German scholar, in a greenish cap,
On his travels "aus Italien," a book of poems, at his feet;
We talked of Robinson's theory of the wild garden,
And the mansions in the castle of St. Theresa's prayer,
Whilst looking at photographs of that mystical wedding,
On the soft, rain-drenched island, as though
Ingmar Bergman were directing *The Tempest*
In modern dress; that extraordinary, flaking,
Green-painted pavilion, the gold-haired guests
In bright plastic anoraks and multi-coloured umbrellas,
Another mirage, another vicarious masque.

Westwell Manor

Over soft, grey-green lavender stalks
A gentle wash of mauve
On grey stone, biscuit stone and honey-coloured gravel.

A seemingly infinite variety of greys,
Then stone paths rucked with amber mosses,
Sharp orange lichens on dry-stone walls.

Soft grey-green to July-juice, apple grey, pigeon breast,
Spattered with tiny white roses
Climbing to studded black moss on the tiles.

Through half-closed eyes, the white Japanese anemones,
White nicotiana, white cane chairs
In the grey-green garden, with the vine clothing

The green-gold south side of the house,
Wisteria leaves palest lime, up
To the softest of soft grey skies, the faint susurrus
Of sycamore trees, beyond them young willows
Encircled with feathery grey-green fern
And the deeper violet of flowering marjoram,

White agapanthus, sundial, herm, obelisk,
Grey-green Chinese bench, dovecote,
Up to the herbaceous border by grass steps

Banked by twisting yews, giant green candlesticks,
And lichen-stained, chamfered, grey-stone spheres;
The north side, plum-grey of South American thunderstorms,

Projects its gable windows between two pines,
Lacking a third in order to declare
Unequivocally its Royalist allegiance.

Anne Finch, Countess of Winchilsea,
Writing in praise of the white foxglove, clinches
The mood, "Warm without sun, grey without rain."

The Rills

After the moonlight garden, the red segment
of moon, blood-stained melon on the horizon,
and Miss Donnithorne's ghost, the rills

down towards the old weed-mantled pond,
(twisted through back-plaited water-ropes),
via seven symmetrical steps

descending, through emerald velvet
turf, limpid curtains of thinnest
water, over algae-bearded stone lips

under an arch of jasmine, green-leafed clematis,
star-flowered wild-blossoming, potato plants,
and a corridor of pleached limes

like one of the structures in Colonna's
Hypnerotomachia; from the milky-green
oxidised lead urns, with tritons and cornucopia

palest variegated spears of iris
flaming in the dappled light, each descent
producing a different note, as the water falls,

churns, pours, streams, dribbles, gurgles
in trillion-noted trickles; two wedge-shaped stone slices
producing a high, clear, even tone,

a curtain of finest water like spun glass,
a mix of very high and very deep notes
a smaller staircase of five stone steps,

holding dead moths and hamadryads' hair,
produces a chuckling, woodland runnel,
the deep tone of wine or milk pouring from a jug.

Six Piano Preludes Of Lennox Berkeley

for Michael Clark

1.
Redrawing the fine lines
of brow, lid, nose and chin
in the insistent, constantly
running streams of finger
movements on the piano

or the more definite chords
on arm, side of head, black-gold hair,
consciously aware
of the objectification
of the desired person

circular leaps
covering the stage
arms crossed behind

for luck
necessary ritual to ward off
this fetishisation of corpses.

2.
Pessimism of mind, optimism of will,
but feebly, although the smile
is brave, aggressive even

the wounded self withdraws
and tries out being calm
in the drugged winter city
all the veins blocked with snow

a silenced memory
of the sea at the end of the street
of tin shacks, rusted girders
the great tidal waves
the grey African sky
because the sound track has been cut off

3.
Quick across the stage
he turns and turns
arms across head
then stretched out directly in front
legs scissored

rolling, turning
on the shiny dance floor
making the pumps squeak

big circular jumps and runs
side-lit sweating face flicks
a fringe of drops flung off
as the head twists quick
yes, bright and smiling

what does the smile know?

4.
Oh, this tune
the slow fall of the melody
insisting against its counter-rise,
unavailingly pulled into the minor key

slow back arch
chest bowed
then arms outstretched
the woman supporting the man

whilst some landscape
yours as much as mine
whispered into your ear alone
spreads out and back inside the retina

curve of the arm
extended, withdrawn slowly
body turns direct to the direct,
untrammelled, or is it threatening,
deep gaze into the eyes.

5.
Together, arms around waists,
a halting, skipping movement
towards the back wall,
the black wall,
through the window
the city snowed up, outside
cold steam rising from the stand pipes

in front,
pressed against the radiators
in grey wool rehearsal clothes
with badges, "I love boys,"
"Heroin is a way of life,"
and "Smile, Jesus loves you!"
in the mirrors of the studio
the backward glance
to check and observe
poised
one leg out

together, hands around waists,
a halting skipping movement
towards the back wall,
the black wall.

6.
That particular place
revealed, the park, the golden pool

sun on arms and shoulders
arms around waists
or lying head to feet
feet to head

leaves above
black carp
and on the golden pool

that particular place
revealed, the park, the golden pool

Porthmeor Beach

For Penny

Down to Lamorna
Past the anemone blanda,
The wind-flowers of the Glynn Valley
And the futuristic cyclamen,
The fifty foot high wind propellers
That march over the road,
And then file back again
As you drive towards them.

Not the pain of the clay workings
The sentinel tin chimneys
Or the Neolithic landscape of Penwith,
But a light drizzle over St. Ives,
The high, wide, pulsing, grey sky of Cornwall again,
The sun struggling beneath it
(An athlete under a blanket)
And the sea, the sea.

Pebble-dashed, white-washed
And slated, tough little, hard-muscled
Granite houses, slyly sexy,
Though Puritan deep down
Under their fisherman's sweaters;
Here in the wet, abandoned streets
Where the old gasworks was, the New Tate
Spiralled ice-cream whiteness and the vista onto the sea.

Porthmeor Beach's cream and ochre sand,
Mauve-silver in the rivulets when wet,
Black rocks then the flat milky-turquoise
And aquamarine sea, navy-blue depths,
Indigo sea-weed, then the little headland
With the chapel, the white finger
Of a lighthouse on the pyramid island,
And behind it all Alfred Wallis's graveyard.

Ben Nicholson must have designed all
The grey and lime-green lichened gravestones
And the toothy wall but not the gents
In the car park covered in wanking surfer graffiti
Scratched on the black paint, as you look back
At the Tate filled and rainbowing with
Bell, Hilton, Wood and Scott,
Heron, Lanyon, Barnes-Graham

And Hepworth, (among the yuccas and tropical
Cornish palms of her middle-town studio,
Turning it into the Antibes of British Modernism),
And dropping down the snail shell inside the Tate
Past the display cases of Leech, Hamada
And Tenmoku glazes, to look out onto
The best painting in the gallery, you say,
Through its helmet visor, the sea.

Port Isaac

Outside the slipway
in the sunlight
opposite the fish market
on the edge of the beach
eating fish and chips
in the sunlight

opposite the fish market
we're in a Christopher Wood
bits of triangular pink and blue
canvas bunting faded grey
by wind and sun and salt
and the beach where the fishermen

let a few cars park
is the natural inlet of the port
the smell of oil, fish and tar
like the wind and sun and salt
on the barnacle encrusted ropes
that tie the lobster pots together
young fishermen and fisherboys
bustle about, Damian, shaved blonde head,
blonde eyelashes, in a green canvas apron,
and a darker boy almost Spanish
long curly hair flopping on his shoulders
thick curving black eyebrows

who puffs his chest out
carries great clear plastic crates
of fish, and the red cheeked fat boy
who helps unload the vans,
and Dennis, the red faced boss
who says to one of his crab-gutters

"Ooh Wendy, you did'n'alf look lovely
In your Brownie uniform!"

Garden, Dove Cottage

Looking at the landscape
through a glass of white wine
from the moss-covered bench;
poppies, bindweed, wild clematis,
tree seedlings from the sycamores,
all extravagantly and generously
overgrown; and surveying the moor,
the Phoenix Tin Mine
and the sharply rising Tor.

The Vermeer light
on the clouds, grey-pink
on the underside, and glowing
with paradise, after the fuller's
ministry, on top;
and behind them the water-
colour pale, Cornish, blue
and the mysterious apple-green
of distances.

The hills are in
their proper place, and the line
of trees delineating fields that change
their cut and pattern seasonally,
combed, crew-cut, plaited, fringed
and bobbed, and drink to Meleager,
the Fury, as you observe the strange
black check on the scarlet silk
of the Snake's Head fritillary.

First Italienne Of Semele At The Archevêché

For William Christie

Like the crowded harbour
of some neo-classical dream city,
(red-gold flakes of light
on the receding waves,
split of apple-green
in pink, mother-of-pearl clouds
reflected on the gilded Corinthian columns),

you do the full colour in "Avert these Omens"...
dry rattling of the rain by lute and timpani,
thunder by portative organ and Baroque drums,
and all the splendour of the storm
accompanied by blockflutes and scurrying strings.

Also sitting in the sunny auditorium,
one of your greatest fans,
the little plump Provencal girl
who plays the harp in the
Place des Martyrs de la Resistance;
Her black hair pulled back into a long ponytail,
her lacy white dress more than a bit old-fashioned -
she might have worn it at her first communion.

Then Ino and Semele in heaven
("Prepare, Prepare..."),
the gushing sister overwhelmed by the flight,
in Congreve's description of interstellar travel.
The words of "Hark the heaven'ly sphere" from
Congreve's poem "On Mrs. Arabella Hunt, Singing";
And Handel would have been amused,
as well as delighted, to note
that Newburgh Hamilton had prepared the lines
"And silence now is drowned in ecstasy of sound"
from a poem by the Rev. Daniel Prat,
Ode to Mr. Handel on his Playing the Organ!

and again the music transmuting everything,
(all that twittering, occasional, verse)
into sound that does indeed
make everything appear divine...

Just at that moment,
as though things had become too perfect,
terrifying problems develop in the feedback,
the "retour du son" on the stage,
crappy electronics and loud speaker levels,
not to mention the clapping of the pigeons' wings,
and the Angelus from Viollet-le-Duc's
restored belfry of Saint Sauveur,
three bells, three bells, nine bells...
"and dwelt among us... "

And you decide to take an orchestral pause.

Volte-Face

For Barney Higson

When you look down the tunnel of someone's eyes
and all you see is him, or her, for miles and miles,
when he looks out of his temple of bone,
observes that human life, like an electric cable,

has innumerable filaments, and why should you imagine
you were just a reincarnation of someone who lived
in the eighteenth century, in a cottage in Somerset,
and had not shared thousands of millions of previous
lives?

His face almost showily, tragically handsome,
a Hellenistic wrestler in a fresco,
eyes only turned to the grey and violet sunset,
sitting, hands on chin, resting elbows on knees,

his cloak furled back and stylishly draped,
or in wide grey flannels, green-striped shirt,
green-gold hair down to his shoulders,
large hands spanning the gleaming saxophone,
or glowing in cricket whites, spattered
and stained with grass, total fluidity
of personality, incarnation or not,
he could be, or become, anyone.

He calls it physics when you think about someone,
and then later the same day, there you are
standing in front of them, looking down the tunnel
of their eyes, seeing only them, for miles and miles.

Sept Prises De Vue Du Grand Banc

1.
A new planted copse on the top,
Olives, young oaks, lavender, arbutus,
And a rather bitter apple tree;
By the rusted clothesline stands, sand pile,
Concrete mixer, and among the small
Wild, crushed, thyme plants,
Scabious and verbena,
Are the little soft-grey and ochre speckled
Cicadas
With the flame-flashing
And turquoise satin flying cloaks;
All the time the thunder prowls around
Waiting to throw ropes of mauve lightning
Into the pool, changing it
From sea-blue to copper-green.

2.
Just suspended beneath
Sprays of withered broom,
The long, empty snakeskin
Is stopped in freeze frame
While the rest of it has moved on;
Made from the finest alchemical plastic,
Each scale exquisitely linked and honey-combed
In palest mauve-brown
And dried-wood silver,
The light now shining
Through the resurrected body.

3.
Here, the gentlest and most English
Of the garden rooms, overgrown grass,
A constellation of wild scabious
One foot above the ground,
Pale pink dog roses walling in one side,
St. John's Wort taking over,
(But able to cure everything, madness,
And even water on the knee),
The two weather-worn memories
Of England, drying
In the Provencal sun,
A Wesleyan chapel bench,
And a horse trough given by Jeremy
Joseph Fry,
A drink to the "friends of man".

4.
As the sun comes up
Over the side of the oak ridge
And hits him full on the side,
You can see that his skin
Is not as white as
The towering spire of alabaster
Bell flowers, rising from the agave;

And that he's even slightly rusty
(In the early oak-leaf golden light)
Particularly round his castration marks,
And where his cloak was once nailed
To his chest; although nothing
Worries him now, in front of the
Neat rows of newly-planted lavender plants,
The olive trees, the spray of broom
And the slim, funeral cypress

5.
In this open-plan house
One wall is the empty space
Between two oak trees,
(Room for a hammock when required)
And gives on to an uninterrupted view
As far as Switzerland (or at least Simiane),
A more civilised view,
(Even though tempestuous and passionate,
Like the one behind Titian's profane Venus,
Than the one from the pool -
The more austere Palestinian version),
Of woods, fields, plains
"With shadowy champains rich'd,"
And lavender planted in hummocky rows,
Like partings in purple hair.

6.
A big stone vase
With Italian Renaissance heads
Of men and women, flowers and garlands,
Birds eating berries in an
Almost abstract design, shells
Under each head, to signal
Their having journeyed as far
As the shrine at Compostela;
A young man with an Errol Flynn cap,
A balding middle-aged man,
A beautiful girl
With her hair tied back.
Stands by two paths
One leading down to the lairs
Of tigers, lions and bears,
The other by a dramatic drop
Into a valley of newly tilled earth,
The whole giant beaker
Seemingly resting on a mill-stone.

7.
By the dining room
Two large wooden doors
Lead into the workshop;
Outside, a large rusting metal
Winch and a plough,
Leggy mallow plants and
Pink hollyhocks,
A little tin bath full of nasturtiums,

And inside the long, low,
Ancient-beamed roof
All the modern sawing
And working equipment you could need.
Drawers full of nails,
Electric router bit sets,
Power drills, fret saws, turning tools,
Saws, planes, vices, chisels,
And at the far end a window looking out
Onto the Luberon hanging on a slant
Like a dark-blue gauze curtain.

The Bedouin Servants Of The Monastery

They celebrate, as Muslims, the feast
of the prophet Moses on the mountain peak
here in the heart of the Sinai
surrounded by the fantastic shapes of red and purple
sandstone (although the sand is white,
as in the temptation of St. Anthony,
minus red-frilled lizard devils);
they also believe in the prophet Aaron,
and the Christian saints Georgius and Katharine,
since they are the descendants of the families
Justinian moved from Anatolia in the year 900
when he built the monastery.

Arriving at sunset
purple sky gashed with unfurling volcanic light,
through mountains parting like curtains,
like draped cloth the grey-mauve mountains
and the white sand slowly turning pink and gold,
as our arrow-car makes for St. Katharine's;
the tall bastion walls of the monastery
purple and gold, surrounded by pencil cypresses,
a garden oasis tended by the monks
and a library housing the Codex Sinaiaticus,
and the Codex Syriacus, the most precious
books outside the Vatican.

The Bedouin servants we meet are young boys
and old men, almost black, squinting in the light,
cracked teeth, turbans, beads, drapes of cloth
against the sand and wind, dyed ropes and shawls,
crouched by the high walls of the monastery
which guards Moses' burning bush, as well as
their special rights sealed by a parchment
with a hand in gold signed by Mahomet,
and a fifth century icon of the head of Jesus
looking as though it were painted yesterday;
they wake you in the middle of the night with camels
to take you to the top of Mount Sinai, to see the dawn.

Damian

waves rolled you
from island to island
trying not to bump your head on rocks
then back to the same shore

grey sea
grey sky
incomprehensible beauty
of a totally grey seascape
water molten pewter
sky delicate grey gradations of pigeon feathers
dark churning water
dark and heavy water-filled clouds overhead
clouds familiar as a mother's face
waves familiar as a father's face
no love like a father's
fading to the thinnest
of pale grey distances
just above
the gun-metal horizon line
grey sky
grey sea

ten years earlier
you had given me the best
parable of the spiritual life
showing me an old radio
whose valves and wires
you had fixed and changed
and got working again

long walks on the edge of the moors
Patrick Brontë's church,
the convent where Robin Hood died,
Charlotte's school now a new one
for disabled children,
the rusting canal
the river filled with dandelion and burdock
talking to boys (now burly husbands),
who had been RAF cadets
when you were the Chaplain at Battyeford

you would have liked it
that Paul the gardener has just married
and has brought his young wife
to live in the Community.

The Widow Of Naim

Dead, but not dead,
Dead to her and to his living core,
Though horribly alive;
Then crashed out on the litter,
Till the man with the black shawl
Over his head for the heat
Walked into the village in a cloud
Of dust, and touched the corpse.

The rejoicing after he had
Delivered her son to her again,
Their visits round the country
To flower-crammed shrines,
Showing friends, "He was dead
And is alive, was lost and is found";
First the husband she loved more than herself,
Then the son, the second time.

She thought about Zechariah
And the widow's son.
God is there very quickly sometimes,
And the second magpie is called Jesus;
Watching this boy, her living dead son,
With the face of a child,
Knowing and corrupted with his sweet smile,
Wearing the little red ribbon for Aids awareness.

Candlemass

One last glance back towards Christmas
And now turn towards the Cross,
The consolation of candles,
The agony of wood and iron.

The black soil is wet,
Pale shoots of bulbs
Push through the beech mast;
Under the vast leafless tree
In the cold eggshell sky
Of this February afternoon,
The new moon is clearly visible
And one star -
A sword at the heart,
Beauty that smarts like sin.

Palm Sunday

On Palm Sunday we are happy
we wave our palms in the air
we rejoice
because You are going to die.

We don't yet know
what it means "to die",
either physically or spiritually,
it's the one thing, sadly,
none of us have ever had any experience of,
maybe that's why we're so happy.

All we know is that You
are going to die "for us",
and we are overjoyed.

We will find out
later in the week
how terrible that really is.

Violin Concerto

For Max

Through the left shoulder blade
The heath, rocks, yellow lichen,
Moths, a snake's skin and through the scales,
On the back of the yellow Morris,
The lid of the boot down, my mother sits
In a yellow dress.

The quest for transcendence,
Unbearable tension, the brass lid
Of the sky firmly clamped down,
With maybe something beyond the shimmer
On the waves'
Silver

Drunkenness as the fiddler plays
And looking deep into the boy's eyes
By the fire, in the wood smoke, and crying.
Grief on the face of the violinist,
Utter desolation, without persona,
In the face of the music, the prodigal father.

Bear And Eagle

For Les Arnold

Over the wave mist two ranks of boats advance,
The paddles command the beat as the brown surge,
White-tipped, splits its light bark.

The amateur ethnologist of the North-West Coast Indians
Balances the tripod on the pebbles; snow-thick fir trees
On the shore-line almost block the sunlight, but
The mahogany camera judders through its tinted celluloid.

A man in a feathered cloak raises his eagle arms,
Up, down, up, down, to the deep song and drumming,
Luring the spirit of the bird.

At the prow of the other, a man in a bear's pelt
Rotates his wooden head in a silent roar
Crippled with earth-bound power.

The camera-man moves to the leather hut,
And films through the log smoke; bear and eagle
Become possessed, their respective essence
Conducted, and the war successfully ritualised.

The amateur ethnologist recoils and then clicks shut,
Preserving the moment deeply, darkly within,
When the bear painfully puts up his paws,
When the eagle exultantly lifts high his wings.

Acrobat

He walks on his hands on the grass,
Deeply tanned, eau-de-nil jogging trousers,
Bright white vest over easy muscle;

Then on the pole-fence by the side of the river
Weaves his arms, almost swims, to balance,
In the watery light, and steady himself.

His lonely eyes betray his shame and pain,
And why he's ostracised by his neighbours,
(For allegedly seducing a pubescent girl)

And occasionally punched and threatened.
Since he'd never met a girl till he was over twenty
His tentative gentleness may have turned sour.

Child-molesting seems a strange term to him
For what happened in that sunlit kitchen
Of the council house, yet it frightens him more

To discover that he is not a child any longer,
And question relentlessly the barbed impediments
That permit him to love only those younger than himself.

Fasching

Herbert has sliced his hand on a mirror
and the long-nosed monsters
dance out of the forest
the tall black dragons
are fake-killed with lots of pigs' blood

from a little concrete balcony
just below the Cathedral
the floats pass by
civic pride, civic generosity
giant papier mache animals
and men, all the political groups
of the town in Napoleonic drag,
(except the skinheads)
tall brass hats, white wigs,
tight white trousers,
on and off horses,
clouds of multi-coloured balloons
marching bands with
terrifying Viking heads
or eagles, millions of boxes
of chocolate cherries, furry toys,
chocolate flowers thrown into the crowd
a float of Chirac with a nuclear
device on his Napoleonic hat
"Typisch Kölsch" fanfare societies,
everybody doing the same thing
at the same time, like Expressionist
theatre or the Nuremberg Rallies

Apollo And The Blackbird

For Jake Macmillan

1.
Poised delicately in the Archaeological Museum
Of Delphi, is a small kylix,
With a black line drawing on white ground,
Of Apollo as a Pythian athlete,
Long-robed like the charioteer,
Long-haired and long-legged,
Sitting on a lion-footed stool,
Kithaera in one hand, while the other
Pours out onto the ground a blood-red libation

But to which gods?

2.
To Demeter, the Mother, who extravagantly
Clothes the mountain that slips down from the shrine,
No longer made of beeswax and birds' wings,
With flowering marjoram and wild yellow daisies,
Or to Artemis, his sister, virgin huntress,
Chasing roe deer, hares and eagles
Up here on the slopes of Parnassos,
And fiercely in love with her brother
Apollo Loxias, the shining one,

Or to older chthonic deities?

3.
Or is the libation for the blackbird
Jauntily perched on a stick in front of him,
As he pours the red wine, the colour of his cloak,
Listening and translating as the bird sings
Looking at him directly in the eye,
As my tame blackbird does here
In the little, leafy garden in Bath,
First from the bright elderberry
On one side of his head then the other

But who is the blackbird?

4.
Is he the black bird of divination and doom
Of bad news, madness, sickness and death?
Or the bird of blessing, time and melancholy
Of friendly, presiding, familial concern?
Making his shrill cheeping warning flights
To guard his children, and teaching us
To imitate his sweetest musical plaints
Knowing that "the sweetest songs
Are those that speak of deepest woe"?

Why does he fix Apollo with his eye?

5.
Is he a she? Watching Apollo Loxias, the Crooked
The oblique and dark-haired sun god, whose eyes
Close drunkenly, more like Dionysos, his brother,
When he smiles, asleep, and whose oracles
Emerge from the Pythia's smoke-filled mouth,
Containing truth, both black and white like lies,
Uttered in the dark from the dusty coils
That writhe and twist together under the temple floor
Where no light ray squeaks through the stone

But what is this riddling lying truth?

6.
Since Apollo is all-knowing,
Although his oracles are oblique,
Only the Pythian witch can tell the real truth
About Koronis, the crow maiden, small
And black-haired, also loved by Apollo
But unfaithful to him, and metamorphosed
By him into a black bird; or was it
The messenger he changed, who spied on her,
The white dove he turned to black

Who brought the news he didn't want to hear?

7.
One version of the legend has Apollo
Rescuing the unborn child, since he couldn't bear
To look at it, the symbol of his love's adultery,
And giving it up to be reared by Chiron
The Centaur, from whose broad black horse's back
The little white baby watched the rushes bend
As he wades in the river, and learns, from Chiron's back
That everything, (rushes, water, sky), is sacred,
And this child grew up to be Asclepius

Did he also learn from the snakes?

8.
Chiron taught him healing, nursing, cooking
And the skill of divination from dreams,
Having dreamt of and slept near coiling
Mating and writhing snakes, and once
He was a man, Asclepius himself
Watched closely while he saw one snake
Cure another with a special herb
And then the pair of them curl round
A single staff, like Hermes' wand caduceus

So why did Zeus the sky god punish him?

9.

Was it for wanting to know who, the man or woman,
Had most pleasure in sex? Or for having dared
To bring back to life a boy who had died,
Although he thought that that was what healing meant?
The delicate cup poised on a floating plastic plate
Also contains its own image in the cup Apollo holds
Perhaps to tell us he is not just the sun god,
But also the poet Pindar celebrating his victory
And commemorating his poem to the young man starting out

And perhaps to the memory of the blackbird?

Domestic Interior

Father,
standing at the foot of the stairs
in an apron, having cleaned
the hostel for "high-grade"
mental patients, from top to toe,
you teach me the meaning of love;

the night before, we had stayed up all night
to watch the moon landing, in the wide
television screen of Buzz Aldrin's helmet,
as well as the Earth, reflected in the blackness:
I see your face, kind, patient, gentle or
convulsed with laughter at Tommy Cooper;

and hear your prayers for fishermen,
or your old sermons, even a funeral address
for Francis Howe, killed like you, on the road.
I don't want to remember, but have no choice,
your head in the mortuary, held in by butter muslin
at the identification,
but see you on the beach
holding Mum up high in your arms,
wearing a huge Mexican straw hat,
or in Jamaica, teaching me English in the morning
Maths in the sweaty afternoon, sometimes,
and in the varnished pine pulpits of Bethels

in Hamburg, Milford Haven, Shipley,
Hull, Norwich and Wyke;
in the garden with an old briar pipe,
the rooks cawing high above Blankeney Grange,
among the leafless trees,
and at Easter dawn, at five o'clock,

among the hundreds of identical white-washed graves
of the Moravian Community;
at Forest Gate with the delinquent East End boys,
who I hero worshipped at the age of seven,
solving the problems of school-leavers
at the Cleckheaton Youth Employment Service,

("No love like a father's"),the heart of love
and how one understands it;
in my dream talking to you
about the location of heaven being made up
of our individual experiences of landscape,
like Ham Hill, all put together, in the sunshine.

Part 3

Hamburg 1947

Two years after the war the Elba froze,
Paraffin heaters in high-ceilinged apartments,
With a spotlight on the Union Jack in the Consulate.

In this photo, my Mum and Dad hold me up,
Wearing my woolly hat, as though they'd just won the cup,
Before placing me carefully on a sledge

That slips down the frozen sides of the Alster
Onto the rumbling black ice of the lake, with two boys
Who become friends for two NAAFI toffees.

Behind the counter in the Flying Angel canteen,
The British Sailors' Society club which my father ran,
I beg the girls, dusty blondes with wraparound plaits,

(Who all ended up on the Reeperbahn),
To take my five year old self to the fair by the bombed
cathedral (rubble to the horizon in frozen waves),

Past the surviving colossus of Hindenberg,
Which hadn't been hit, past the leafless trees
And the grim pier where Jewish survivors

Huddle to catch the boat for Israel;
But I am more interested in the dodgems,
The waltzers and the rickety roller–coaster.

I am allowed to stay up for the Variety Show
In the Club (not the one in the Hansa Theatre where
Rollerskated acrobats whirl on towers of tables,

And fat white-faced clowns sit on a sequinned moon
Listing all the food no longer available), but the one
In my father's Club with Helma Kelian

And her all-girl accordion band with flowers in their
  hair,
And Tiger Lily, the terrifying contortionist,
And the elderly Adagio dancers who swoop and whirl

In the spotlight like fighter planes, to the
  accompaniment
Of the elegant Herr Giesenberg, ex-Nazi, first violin
Of the German Radio orchestra, who gives my
  mother

German lessons for a bag of coffee.
Now in Hagedorn Straße, where we used to live,
Fifty years later, the dustbins are in exactly
The same place, though boxed in with concrete lids,
But still under the same chestnut trees,
And I can see myself in the front bay window

Dipping toast soldiers in a fresh boiled egg
Looking out at the beggar (where I'm standing now),
Who scrapes the side of a baked bean tin

With a spoon, and my mother lets me go
From our fragrant paraffin warmth
To give him bread in the snow.

When I had, successively, asthma and hooping cough
And lay in bed with scarring kaolin poultices,
My father showed me silent films on the wall

From Herr Peck's Studio, old Riefenstahl films
Of the Olympics, which I wanted again and again,
With their kitsch fascist fantasy of ancient Greek life

And divers diving endlessly from the high diving
    board
In slow motion, and animated tales from Grimm
Like The Boy Who Wanted to Know What Fear Was

With its Semitic ghouls and monsters.
My mum's cleaning help, and sometimes my nanny,
Is Ursula, whose uncle lives at the end of a sunflower
    field

Who she would take me to visit in his wooden hut;
It had an earth floor, but after the endless winter
It was suddenly hot, airless, with the floor baked dry,
Sunlight piercing through the wooden slats, and the
    room
Divided in quarters by blankets and sheets on ropes;
Ursula and I sit on the doorstep shelling peas

Looking at the sunflowers, then, only one month later
Her uncle cut his throat with a cut-throat razor,
Unable to cope with the aftermath of war.

My best friend lives in the flat below us,
The caretaker's son, whose mother asked mine
If she could "become the bath", the tin bath

Which we all shared; and he and I play together
With my beautiful model of a Hamburg tram
Whose roof comes off revealing all the tiny people

Who frequently drop out and fall through the cracks
Of the open veranda floor, then having picked them
up
We mooch about by the ruined fountain

At the bottom end of the garden, with its statue
Of another little boy, standing on a plinth
Wreathed in rusty wire and covered in weeds.

Wyke 1950

Since I'd just come from Germany, and even spoke
A little German (having played the wolf in
"Rotkepchen"
So well at the Army Primary School, that another boy's
mother,

Sitting next to mine, thought it unfair that a German
boy
Was allowed the best part while the others struggled),
But my Yorkshire Primary School friends

Threw my mac on the floor of the cloakroom and called
me "Nazi!"
Though they all wrote their names on the inside
Of the Illustrated Bible they presented to me

When we left for Jamaica Derry Barlow, Brian Raistrick
And my new best friend, Elizabeth Shoesmith,
With whom I used to swap clothes quite regularly

And have our photos taken, was particularly keen
When I dressed as a Chinaman in the Summer Pageant-
I can still smell the Leichner greasepaint Auntie Nellie
put on me.

Although close to Bradford it was a rural existence,
Scrubby thistle-strewn fields with dangerous wells and
pit shafts,
And behind the Manse, the Yorkshire Moors

Where Moira our Irish setter flame-streaked in the
wind,
Past walls of Yorkshire ironstone, soot-stained with age,
And all the mill chimneys, and the little stone terraces,

Where Auntie Nellie lived, and Blankeney Grange,
Already an Old Peoples' Home, surrounded by tall
Leafless beeches squatted by a colony of rooks

Who cawed all day like old machinery, and who I heard
When I had to go to bed early in the summer,
Watching the pattern of leaves projected by sunset

On the bedroom wall; we lived in the heart
Of a Moravian Community, with rapturous
And liturgically ecstatic services,

Like Zinzendorf's Christingles, and Easter morning
Services at daybreak, in the cemetery
Of identical white-washed gravestones.

Every Sunday lunch Dorothy came,
Moravian sharing being a mystical tradition
As much as Zwingli and Zinzendorf,
A widow in black, with stone-coloured stockings,
Stone-coloured face and hair, talking about Fulneck
College and white-washing the graves.

And while she gossiped about the Mallinsons
And the saga at the farm, I dreamt of the green and gold
Ballet dress in Auntie Nellie's dressing-up box,

Smelling magically of scent and sweat,
And about sleeping in her daughter Sheila's bed
Since I was only eight, or listening to the rooks

In the tall bare trees in Blankeney Grange,
After picking up and classifying the burnt-out
Cardboard casings of last night's fireworks.

Forest Gate 1951

Out of the gate to the swimming baths,
Past the smell of privet flowers and cat piss,
Then the echoey shouts, snorts and seal-sounds

Which stir the stomach, rebounding from
The glass skylight, the ochre glazed brick
And cracked white tiles of the Victorian pool,

Everyone wearing old woolly swimming trunks
With frayed elastic waists, and in cubicles
Rough army serge, rough army surplus.

Afterwards across the scrubland, through bushes,
Stomach tightening, into the ruined garage, clambering up
From the wrecked billiard table with its ripped baize

And plaster covered broken slate,
Into a tiny room where my grown-up newest friend
Tries to force himself into me with the aid
Of a small tin of Vaseline, lying on his old pale mac;
And as he comes between my legs, gritty, wet,
And sweet, because I think he likes me,

I feel quite grown up, like Gordon, Liam, Trivet
And Ginger Mounty, and other apprentice
Gangland kids, only late teens, with their ginger stubble,

But to me grown men, their sex, Brylcreemed hair,
Balls, thick legs, cocks and smell, compel as I watch
Fascinated in the steamed-up mirrors

Glimpses of naked bodies, great bushes of pubic hair
As they get into deep baths, or slip into lavatory lock-ups
Or hide in the back garden of the Remand Home my father ran.

With a couple of primary school friends we built our own
Stage with a swishing curtain between the trees,
And having seen Alice at a local theatre

I designed costumes for a Betty Grable figure
In thick wax crayons, and disappeared down
The rabbit hole of literature and fantasy.

I also dealt in cigarette cards, the sumptuous delight
Of sets of film stars, racing horses or household hints,
And once, having lost all my collection

In a legitimate game, I broke into my friend's house,
A nine year old thief, through the French window
From the garden, and stole them all back again
Along with several little scent bottles,
And an eyelash curler, that I found in the drawer
Of his mother's dressing-table.

Hull 1953

In the Library Stack are the coveted art books
"Kouroi", "Michelangelo", "Indian Temple Sculpture"
Which I'm allowed to take home and copy with pen and
pencil;

My father and I go to the Library together,
And we can also borrow long-playing records
Of Conchita Supervía singing Carmen,

Sibelius Symphonies, which haunt me still,
As well as thrilling but incomprehensible novels
Like *Ulysses, Point Counter Point* and *Antic Hay*.

The Library opens up everything school closed down,
art, music and literature, although playing Miranda
In *The Tempest* in a single sex Private School

Offers varied delights and various friendships
Like Eric Barkworth, a dark-skinned Indian Prince,
Whose mother owned a fleet of fishing trawlers
And whose brother Trevor (who I worshipped
In a different way, owned a TR3, and drove me home
After Eric and I had been playing together.

Eric had a set of black Caruso 78s, (maybe his dead
father's?),
Which we played endlessly, as well as a
Squat Grundig Tape machine, on which we recorded

Our radio plays, sometimes completely our own
Invention, and sometimes scenes from Penguin
Editions of Tennessee Williams and Sophocles.

Eric was a boy of limitless fantasy,
And quickly became a soulmate as dear
As Neil was to become seven years later.

The other fantasy world was opened up
By the cinema, where I used to persuade
My Auntie Grace, with whom I lived for a few months,

To take me to see, with Eric, *The Great Caruso,*
Arthur and the Knights of the Round Table
And *The Beautiful Blonde From Bashful Bend.*

Norwich 1954

Mckenna was another kind of friend – we rediscovered
Sex together in a simple, functional way, behind
The green-painted door of the playground lavatories,

Although he wasn't interested in Handel's Water Music,
Or the school Shakespeare performance,
Where we sat in the dark, holding each others' hands

Or in each others' trousers, gawping at the sixth former
In mauve tights playing Orsino in *Twelfth Night*,
Or at the revelation of Nugent Monk's *Macbeth*

At the Maddermarket Theatre, which shook me to the
core,
With its mixture of Fifties Modernism
And Elizabethan Revival, showing me

A New Way to be Happy, until I was confirmed
After lengthy preparation classes, by the Bishop of
Norwich;
And once I'd read Pater's *Marius* a few years later

I knew how he felt, and my moments of religious
intuition,
Where mystical apprehensions of the queerness of the
Universe,
(Sunlight on the red-brick wall in the late afternoon,

The earth shaking, or seeing myself from the bedroom
    ceiling),
Made me become a server at the Anglo-Catholic
    Church
On the edge of the countryside, at seven in the
    morning,

The sharp smell of the communion wine in the
    Sacristy,
Listening to the formulaic confession of the tall, fair-
    haired priest,
Pouring water over his fingers and afterwards drying
    them

Then sitting in the choir-stalls, in love with
One of the dark-haired older choirboys, who used to
    wink at me,
Staring firmly through the stain-glass windows at the
    moving leaves.

Auxerre, 1955

To teenagers now
we would appear very cool,
only ten years after the war
English kids in Fifties France,
collars of our blazers up, big skirts,
wide black belts, Brylcreemed quiffs
and sunglasses, but not as cool
as our French penfriends
with their Brando Roman haircuts
listening to Lionel Hampton and
Sidney Bechet, on white plastic
record players, or Françoise Hardy
on huge jukeboxes in little sunlit
town square cafés.

François, coolest, blondest,
with his three brothers, Serge,
small and dark like his mother,
Gilles with glasses, reading about
the bottom of the Mediterranean,
and little Alain; as well as their father,
Docteur Besle, two packs of Gitanes a day,
and adorable mother, with whom I
used to read Ionesco, just out
in Gallimard, sumptuous cream
paper with thin scarlet lines,
or Beckett in Editions de Minuit
bright white paper, navy-blue printed titles
and a little Cocteauesque pentagram star.

And the sunlight over the river Yonne,
deep shadows of the poplars in the water,
magical as Pisarro; the public swimming bath,
and water-skiing seeming as sophisticated
to us Yorkshire kids as St. Tropez,
Francoise Sagan or Bernard Buffet.
All we did was hang round the coffee bars
till sex reared its head during the slow
dances at "surprise parties", or dancing
in the pointed gabled attic where Yvonne lived,
the Doctor's maid, with her light moustache,
and Algerian boyfriend, who taught us to tango,
to drink blonde beer, and pretend to be drunk in order
to lurch into each others' arms for our first kiss.

Eromenos

On this red-figured vase
I proffer my gift to you, a hare,
To encourage your interest in hunting,
And a fighting cock,
To satisfy your enjoyment of manly pleasures,

A string bag containing gymnasium equipment,
Astragaloi, to develop your already hard body,
And money in a little leather purse,
For whatever you wish, as well as
A flower to celebrate your beauty;

With my other hand I touch your chin,
Brush your cheeks with the tips of my fingers,
Wrapped up as you are in a white cloak to your neck,
As though you've just come out of the sea, or a bath,
Even though you still smell of wood smoke;

"Ho pais kalos" is written above your image
A sufficient reason, since this love
Gives birth to ideas and ideals,
While the love between men and women
Gives birth to bodies.

Bearded erastes, beardless eromenos
But with clearly delineated sideburns;
The rules are that you must not show desire
The most you can demonstrate is anteros,
Affection – no problem.

Sayat Nova

For Boris

Praise beauty
Wherever it is found!

Your face is a glimpse of Paradise beyond!
Your body a foretaste of eternal delight!

The Armenian poet notes how
Pomegranate juice spreads through white linen,

How out-of-water fish flick on a pewter tray.
Thorns. Thorns. Thorns.

As the lightning flashes soundlessly
Rain drenches the ancient books

Positioned in rows on the monastery roof to dry.
The wind turns a thousand leaves

The wind turns a thousand leaves together,
To hear the crackling of the vellum leaves
As they turn,
While the grey sky stretches out behind.

I rejoice to praise beauty
Wherever it is found,

For example in the feet of men
Pressing the drenched carpets

Fixing the dye
Fox-red, indigo and red-purple

Wool, freshly dyed, wet and steaming,
Slate-blue, violet, black and ochre,

For the rich Turkey carpets
Made in Georgia.

A man slyly covers a white cockerel's wing
With blood-scarlet dye,

While in a vision St. George on horseback
Steps neatly by against the lime-washed tombs,

Past white cockerels with scarlet combs,
And a large-eyed boy dressed in scarlet.

On the domed uneven roof of the Hammam
The boy watches men covered in mud

Being showered from a high ledge
By naked attendants with copper ewers.

On a table are bowls of lemons,
Pomegranates, saffron flowers and eggs.

The bridegroom is ceremonially cleansed
Standing naked in a flat copper bath.

His head is shaved, but not his eyebrows
Which join together, and his eyes are lined

With indigo kohl.
Scented water is poured all over him

Which runs down his broad, flat chest
With rose petals, orange and saffron blossom.

The Poet at the Prince's Court
Leads the prayers before the Hunt;

White-mauve face, an encrusted icon,
Looks at the brutal man with peacock feathers

In his black, felt turban, sneering beneath
His first moustache, and slowly smiles,

A live peacock draped across his shoulder,
Its beak in his mouth drinking his saliva,

His scarlet waistcoat open on his tanned chest.
Written on burnt black paper

The poem disappears:
"You deserted us, and retreated,

But we spun a cocoon around you,
So that you might emerge

As a butterfly
In your new life".

Words are powerless in your presence
Your face is like a rose.

As the poet enters the monastery
The sky is pitch black, although the sun shines,

The church stone is grey-ochre, hit
By bright, low, storm splashed sunlight.

"Now the joy of nuptials, now grief,
Now feasting and rejoicing.

If you create through a free spirit,
There can be no decay."

What is the sound of twenty black-clothed monks
Chewing pomegranates? Ear-shattering!

The brothers wash each others' feet
Then lift them up completely,

Drape them over their shoulders
So as not to dirty their soles before going grape pressing.

A white ass turns the stone olive press.
A huge mound of olives, makes a noise

Like mussels, like shingle, then the waves
Of rich, gold, olive oil. Green-gold.

Boys chant as the poet digs his grave,
As he does so the church fills with sheep,

Crowding round the black grave in the nave.
A bronze hand is placed on his sleeping brow,

As he dreams about his parents and his youth.
A golden ball swings from the black-blindfolded angel

Back to the large-eyed boy, while the father
Is still dewed with steam in the Hammam,

Lying, looking at him in the high, white Arabic room,
Where the carpets are woven, which is suddenly filled

With angels and great piles of uncarded wool,
Like clouds that have been grounded.

Outside are the poplars, which his mother thinks
Are the most unfriendly trees, because they offer

No shade to the traveller,
Or branch room for the birds.

The poet leaves the monastery,
And the tower descends by itself

Onto the basilica; the poet
Descends a ladder with his lute,

Long-necked and covered with
Mother of pearl.

Artemesia

In The Allegory of Painting
You have fallen to the ground,
As though in a narcoleptic trance,
Your square palette, your brushes
Are scattered around you on the floor,
And yet your face looks rested,
Dreaming, under the swathe of brown-gold brocade;

Otherwise you are naked
And the red mask of tragedy
Has slipped from your face
And lies by your side on the studio floor.

How do we interpret this?
How did you mean us to interpret this?
How do you interpret this?

Another dreadful memory of your rape?
Flung to the ground and ravished
In the middle of painting your self-portrait?
The futility of art in the face
Of psychic trauma?
The blissful content of having finished
Another day's work satisfactorily?

Plûtot Catholique

I can hear your boy's gruff, slightly monotone, voice
As though it were next to me, saying
"Plutôt Catholique", as I asked about
Your Primary School at St. Thomas's
And your secondary school next to the
Side entrance of the cathedral,
L'Ecole de Fustel de Coulanges,
Beneath the statue of Notre Dame
Where you used to play your accordions at break time.

As I sit and watch the sun come up
Behind the vast stained-glass Apocalypse windows
In Milan Cathedral wine-coloured, brown, orange, red
Scenes of the Resurrection and Crucifixion
And at the end of the mass contemplate
How symbol and metaphor pervade the mystery
Truer than most science
And look at the whorls of red, white and black
Marble on the chapel floor,

Stone from the beginning of the universe,
And think of the two times in operation,
Human time and God's time;
Hippolyte Taine first noted
That when the light enters,
Transformed by the yellow and purple
Stained glass windows, it seems filtered
Through the ruddy and orangey colours
Of autumn leaves.

Hadrian To Antinous

Everything is metaphor
The sweep of the dragon's tail
That knocks the stars from the sky,
Your boy's face and body, athletic,
Curled with fine iulan down
Covering your skin, deep grey eyes,
Delicate fingers, that play the kithara;

Turning your back to me
In order to sleep better, but putting
My hands on your belly, then
Turning back again in an infantile embrace,
The best sleep of all;
The moments before the hunt
Resting and walking in the forest

Are the episodes of which
I have the clearest memory -
The stillness in the sun-dappled glades
The mossy floor covered in pine needles,
The scent of the wind in the pines
Like swimming pools and the sea
And you lying asleep with your arm over your eyes

Showing me your under arms
Which I want to lap and bury my face in,
Like a hunting dog, as I do with the soft taut skin
At the back of your knees;
An apple-green sky through the trees as twilight thickens
To mauve-grey, and distant rumbles of thunder force us
To smell the rain on the wet dust.

David And Goliath

You have beheaded me;
You have grasped my depraved, seriously hung over,
Sexually obsessed, head by its greasy hair
And swung your sword
Over your naked shoulders
Where the bag with pebbles and the sling are kept;
Your trousers are open provocatively

At the crotch, but your string belt
Keeps your shirt tucked in
Covering your modesty;
Your expression, paradoxically, is rather reflective,
Even tender; you don't regret the unbelievably violent
act much,
And you might even forget about it quite soon,
But there's a lot of life to get on with…

Saul, Jonathan,
Becoming king,
Writing psalms,
Not to mention Bathsheba,
Uriah, it might all
Get quite difficult,
Who knows?

Blackbird

I think the dead
Come back to us as birds
The eternal return

Not the firebirds
And swan princesses
Of myth and fairy tale

But, for example,
The blackbird
Who cocks her head to one side

Like my mother,
As if to say
Do you really think so?

Or as the collar dove
Who sits in the guttering
Above the bedroom window

Like my friend Anthea
Murmuring only warm
And encouraging sounds.

British Museum Drawings

The Fra Angelico drawing of King David
Is a reflection of you
The Stephano da Verona drawing of Charity
Is a reflection of you
The Pisanello drawing of the hanged men
(When I think of your eyes and mouth
Like those of the boy at the foot of the drawing of 1434
Looking straight at us
While his mother looks to the side
Is a reflection of you)
The rope around their necks
Turning them to provolone cheeses,
Their socks around their ankles
Kicked down as their legs thrashed
At the moment of death;
The Gozzoli drawing of a naked man
With a horse, sketched from the sculpture
Of the dioscuri – the horse tamers – in Rome
Is a reflection of you,
The Pollaiuolo Adam
Is a reflection of you
The Mantegna Saint James on the way to execution
Is a reflection of you
With one soldier pushing another
Up against a wall, while behind them,
Almost involuntarily,
St. James performs his miracle,
And the Mantegna drawing of a sleeping man
On a stone slab – like a sketch for the foreshortened Christ

Is a reflection of you
The Allegory of the Fall of Ignorant Humanity
Is a reflection of you
Leonardo's head of a woman
With her hair as the landscape
Is a reflection of you
As is the boy Christ
Playing tenderly with a cat;
Verrocchio's head of an angel
Has stolen your mouth
And Carpaccio's Saint George
Where you feel sorry for the dragon
Is still a reflection of you

Roman Bath

Lying on the side of the tepid pool
Looking up at the vaulted hollow tiles
And out at the far end which opens
Onto an English landscape of oak-covered hills
Larch, holm oak, holly, elder, willow and flowering thorn

One or two leaves have blown in onto the water
The reflections play over your young white body
Firm and muscled as a gymnast, and on the hair
On your chest, underarms, legs
Turning them to gold wire

At the other end of the pool
Splashes and shouts of other bathers;
You half-listen as you dream of the girl
In Ireland when your regiment moved away
Your face is expressionless

When I saw the fresco
One sun-baked afternoon in Pompeii
Of the basket of figs
I knew they were as beautiful
And delicious as you

Warehouse

An old man's love
Is a strange commodity
For a boy without an abacus;
Useless, pointless,
Incalculable, hopeless

I have several
Rickety wooden warehouses
Full of it, above the piano,
Shelf on shelf, rather disordered,
Waiting for your inspection

After our dialectical discussion
(Now that you have emerged
From the gymnasium,
Glistening with sweat,
And smelling sweetly of grass).

After Michelangelo

(Sonnets To Emilio De' Cavalieri)

1
If desire of immortality,
Which elevates and directs men's thoughts,
Could make my feelings clear to you,
It would perhaps make you merciful,
You who still rule over me
In the house of love.

But since, according to divine law,
The soul has an endless life
While the body, after a brief existence, dies
Our senses can neither fully praise
Nor describe the soul's worth,
Nor fully understand it.

Alas then, how shall the chaste lusts
Which set my heart on fire
Be heard or made clear
By those who always
See themselves through others,
Since I am shut off from you, the man I love

And shut out of your sweet company,
While you still listen,
And are forced to hear, the lies about me?
And to say the truth,
He who doesn't believe them
Is a liar himself.

2
If one chaste love
Or one amazing act of pity,
Or if one equal fate should strike
Two lovers equally,
If one will and spirit
Governs two hearts

And if one soul in two bodies
Is made eternal,
Lifting both to heaven
On one pair of wings,
And if love with one golden arrow
Burns and burrows

In the deepest recesses
Of two bosoms,
And two equal hearts,
And if each loves the other
And neither himself
With equal desire, and equal delight

With the ultimate aim
That both direct their wishes
To the self-same object or affect,
And if all this
Were multiplied by a thousand,
It would not achieve

A hundredth part of the love and fidelity
That I feel for you,
Which only the most
Ultimate disdain
Could ever break
Or resolve.

3
You know that I know,
My darling, that you know
That I come here
To delight in being close to you,
And you know that I know
That you know who I really am indeed.

Why then do we hesitate
To greet each other properly,
Even now, if the hope that you gave me is true?
Let the wall be broken down
Between these two truths, since this hidden
Problem has gained a double force.

If I were to love only in you
What you love in yourself,
Do not, on that account, despise me,
Since it is simply one spirit
Loving another in your beautiful face, which is
What I long for as well as what I see and find.

And this is something
Misunderstood by ordinary minds,
But if they really wanted
To understand it,
Then the only way they could
Would be to have to die first.

4
If I could have believed
That knowing you at first sight,
At the first glance of your soul,
(A dazzling phoenix flying into the sun),
I would be able to renew myself at your fire
In which my whole and entire being burns,

Or like the swiftest lynx, or hart or leopard,
Fleeing from its natural prey
And seeking its own good,
That I would have run after your actions
Opinions, smiles, virtuous words -
What would I have done?

Why should I lament? Since in the eyes
Of the blessed angel (who you are),
You alone hold my peace, rest and salvation;
Perhaps when I was young it would have been wrong for me
To have met you, since only now you give me such an impulse
To fly on wings, to follow wherever your goodness leads me.

* 9 7 8 1 7 8 0 3 5 4 8 8 0 *

ND - #0182 - 060826 - C0 - 203/127/13 - PB - 9781780354880 - Gloss Lamination